HEINEMANN MODULAR MATHEMATICS
for EDEXCEL AS AND A-LEVEL
Revise for
Decision Maths 2

John Hebborn

Heinemann

Edexcel
Success through qualifications

D1353988

Heinemann Educational Publishers,
a division of Heinemann Publishers (Oxford) Ltd,
Halley Court, Jordan Hill, Oxford, OX2 8EJ

OXFORD   MELBOURNE   AUCKLAND   JOHANNESBURG
BLANTYRE   GABORONE   PORTSMOUTH NH (USA)   CHICAGO

First published 2002

05   04   03   02
10   9   8   7   6   5   4   3   2   1

ISBN 0 435 51131 9

Cover design by Gecko Limited

Original design by Geoffrey Wadsley; additional design work by Jim Turner

Typeset and illustrated by Tech-Set Limited, Gateshead, Tyne and Wear

Printed in Great Britain by Scotprint

Acknowledgements:

The publisher's and author's thanks are due to Edexcel for permission to
reproduce questions from past examination papers. These are marked with an [E].

The answers have been provided by the author and are not the responsibility of
the examining board.

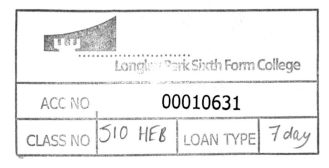

About this book

This book is designed to help you get your best possible grade in your Decision Maths 2 examination. The series authors are Chief and Principal examiners and moderators, and have a good understanding of Edexcel's requirements.

Revise for Decision Maths 2 covers the key topics that are tested in the Decision Maths 2 exam paper. You can use this book to help you revise at the end of your course, or you can use it throughout your course alongside the course textbook; *Heinemann Modular Mathematics for Edexcel AS and A-level Decision Mathematics 2*, which provides complete coverage of the syllabus.

Helping you prepare for your exam

To help you prepare, each topic offers you:

- **Key points to remember** – summarise the mathematical ideas you need to know and be able to use.

- **Worked examples and examination questions** – help you understand and remember important methods, and show you how to set out your answers clearly.

- **Revision exercises** – help you practise using these important methods to solve problems. Answers are given at the back of the book so you can assess your progress.

- **Test yourself questions** – help you see where you need extra revision and practice. If you do need extra help they show you where to look in the *Heinemann Modular Mathematics for Edexcel AS and A-level Decision Mathematics 2* textbook.

Exam practice and advice on revising

Examination style practice paper – this paper at the end of the book provides a set of questions of examination standard. It gives you an opportunity to practise taking a complete exam before you meet the real thing. The answers are given at the back of the book.

How to revise – for advice on revising before the exam, read the **How to revise** section on the next page.

How to revise using this book

Making the best use of your revision time

The topics in this book have been arranged in a logical sequence so you can work your way through them from beginning to end. But **how** you work on them depends on how much time there is between now and your examination.

If you have plenty of time before the exam then you can **work through each topic in turn**, covering the key points and worked examples before doing the revision exercises and test yourself questions.

If you are short of time then you can **work through the Test yourself sections first**, to help you see which topics you need to do further work on.

However much time you have to revise, make sure you break your revision into short blocks of about 40 minutes, separated by five- or ten-minute breaks. Nobody can study effectively for hours without a break.

Using the Test yourself sections

Each Test yourself section provides a set of key questions. Try each question:

- If you can do it and get the correct answer then move on to the next topic. Come back to this topic later to consolidate your knowledge and understanding by working through the key points, worked examples and revision exercises.

- If you cannot do the question, or get an incorrect answer or part answer, then work through the key points, worked examples and revision exercises before trying the **Test yourself** questions again. If you need more help, the cross-references beside each **Test yourself** question show you where to find relevant information in the *Heinemann Modular Mathematics for Edexcel AS and A-level Decision Mathematics 2* textbook.

Reviewing the key points

Most of the key points are straightforward ideas that you can learn: try to understand each one. Imagine explaining each idea to a friend in your own words, and say it out loud as you do so. This is a better way of making the ideas stick than just reading them silently from the page.

As you work through the book, remember to go back over key points from earlier topics at least once a week. This will help you to remember them in the exam.

Transportation problems

Key points to remember

1 The number of occupied cells (routes used) must be equal to one less than the sum of the number of rows and the number of columns.

2 The **shadow costs** R_i, for the ith row, and K_j, for the jth column, are obtained by solving $R_i + K_j = C_{ij}$ for **occupied cells**, taking $R_1 = 0$ arbitrarily.

3 The **improvement index** I_{ij} for an **unoccupied cell** is defined by

$$I_{ij} = C_{ij} - R_i - K_j$$

4 If all improvement indices are **greater than or equal to zero** then an **optimal solution** has been reached.

5 A **closed path** or **loop** is a sequence of cells in the transportation tableau such that:

(i)   each pair of consecutive cells lies in either the same row or the same column
(ii) no three consecutive cells lie in the same row or column
(iii) the first and last cells of a sequence lie in the same row or column
(iv) no cell appears more than once in the sequence.

6 A feasible solution to a transportation problem is **degenerate** if the number of used cells is less than the magic number $(m + n - 1)$, where m is the number of rows and n is the number of columns.

Example 1
A charter airline has 22 planes of the same type. At the end of a weekend operation the planes are located as follows:
4 in London (L), 12 in Barcelona (B) and 6 in Athens (A).
For the next stage of operation the planes are required in three other cities as follows:
5 in Copenhagen (C), 10 in Paris (P) and 7 in Stuttgart (S).

The flying distances between the starting points and the destinations are, to the nearest 100 miles:

	C	P	S
L	600	200	500
B	1100	500	600
A	1800	1300	1200

The airline wishes to redistribute the planes so that the total flying distance is a minimum. Give this minimum distance.

Answer

The transportation tableau for this problem is:

From \ To	C	P	S	Planes available
L	600	200	500	4
B	1100	500	600	12
A	1800	1300	1200	6
Planes required	5	10	7	

The total number of planes available is:

$$4 + 12 + 6 = 22$$

The total number of planes required is:

$$5 + 10 + 7 = 22$$

Since (the number of planes required) = (the number of planes available), the problem is a balanced problem.

The north-west corner solution is:

	C	P	S	
L	4			4
B	1	10	1	12
A			6	6
	5	10	7	

To test for optimality we need to calculate first the shadow costs R_i and K_j using **2** and then the improvement indices I_{ij} for the unoccupied cells.

Using
$$R_i + K_j = C_{ij}$$
2

for the occupied cells gives:

cell (1, 1): $R_1 + K_1 = 600$
cell (2, 1): $R_2 + K_1 = 1100$
cell (2, 2): $R_2 + K_2 = 500$
cell (2, 3): $R_2 + K_3 = 600$
cell (3, 3): $R_3 + K_3 = 1200$

Taking $R_1 = 0 \Rightarrow K_1 = 600$, $R_2 = 500$, $K_2 = 0$, $K_3 = 100$ and $R_3 = 1100$.

Using
$$I_{ij} = C_{ij} - R_i - K_j \qquad \boxed{3}$$

for the unoccupied cells gives:

cell $(1, 2)$: $I_{12} = 200 - 0 - 0 = 200$
cell $(1, 3)$: $I_{13} = 500 - 0 - 100 = 400$
cell $(3, 1)$: $I_{31} = 1800 - 1100 - 600 = 100$
cell $(3, 2)$: $I_{32} = 1300 - 1100 - 0 = 200$

Since all the I_{ij} values are non-negative this solution is optimal. The transportation pattern is then:

send   4 planes from London to Copenhagen
        1 plane from Barcelona to Copenhagen
        10 planes from Barcelona to Paris
        1 plane from Barcelona to Stuttgart
        6 planes from Athens to Stuttgart

The minimum distance is then:

$$(4 \times 600) + (1 \times 1100) + (10 \times 500) + (1 \times 600) + (6 \times 1200)$$
$$= 16\,300 \text{ miles}$$

Example 2

The transport manager of a company has three factories, A, B and C, and three warehouses, 1, 2 and 3. He wishes to determine which factory should supply each warehouse so as to minimise total transportation costs. In a given month, the supply requirements of each warehouse, the production capacities of the factories and the cost of shipping one unit of product on each possible route are shown in the table below.

		Warehouse			
		1	**2**	**3**	Available
	A	5	3	7	70
Factory	**B**	7	5	4	40
	C	10	7	3	40
	Demand	80	30	40	

(a) Determine a minimum cost transportation pattern and give the minimum cost.
(b) Find another transportation pattern with this same minimum cost.

Answer

(a) The north-west corner solution is:

	1	2	3	Available
A	70			70
B	10	30		40
C			40	40
Demand	80	30	40	

This solution is degenerate as only four cells are occupied. When we place 30 in cell (2, 2) we satisfy both a row constraint and a column constraint. We therefore place a zero in cell (3, 2) and regard this cell as occupied. We can then use the usual formula **2** to calculate the R and K values. The results are:

	$K_1 = 5$	$K_2 = 3$	$K_3 = -1$
$R_1 = 0$	X $\quad$ [5]	[3]	[7]
$R_2 = 2$	X $\quad$ [7]	X $\quad$ [5]	[4]
$R_3 = 4$	[10]	X $\quad$ [7]	X $\quad$ [3]

where X indicates an occupied cell.

The improvement indices for the unoccupied cells are:

$$I_{12} = 3 - 0 - 3 = 0$$
$$I_{13} = 7 - 0 - (-1) = 8$$
$$I_{23} = 4 - 2 - (-1) = 3$$
$$I_{31} = 10 - 4 - 5 = 1$$

As there are no negative improvement indices this transportation pattern has minimum cost. The pattern is:

send
$\qquad\qquad$ 70 from A to 1
$\qquad\qquad$ 10 from B to 1
$\qquad\qquad$ 30 from B to 2
$\qquad\qquad$ 40 from C to 3

The minimum cost is:

$$(70 \times 5) + (10 \times 7) + (30 \times 5) + (40 \times 3) = 350 + 70 + 150 + 120$$
$$= 690$$

(b) Since $I_{12} = 0$ we can find an alternative solution with the same minimum cost by using route (1, 2). The required loop is:

X⁻	⌐ i	
X∟	⌐ !X	
	X	X

Adding and subtracting θ as required we have:

$70 - \theta$	θ	
$10 + \theta$	$30 - \theta$	
		40

We chose θ to be as large as possible, in this case $\theta = 30$. We then obtain:

40	30	
40		
		40

The pattern is then:

send

40 from A to 1
30 from A to 2
40 from B to 1
40 from C to 3

The cost of this pattern is also 690.

Example 3

A transportation problem involves the following costs, supply and demand:

From \ To	D_1	D_2	Supply
S_1	6	4	10
S_2	6	7	30
S_3	5	8	40
Demand	20	40	

(a) Show that the problem is unbalanced and draw a transportation tableau for the corresponding balanced problem.
(b) Write down the north-west corner solution and then use the stepping-stone method to obtain an optimal solution.
(c) Interpret your optimal solution and obtain the minimum cost.

Answer

(a) Number of units available: $10 + 30 + 40 = 80$
Number of units required: $20 + 40 = 60$
So the problem is unbalanced.

The transportation tableau for the corresponding balanced problem is:

	D_1	D_2	Dummy D_3	Supply
S_1	6	4	0	10
S_2	6	7	0	30
S_3	5	8	0	40
Demand	20	40	20	

(b) The north-west corner solution is:

	D_1	D_2	D_3	Supply
S_1	10			10
S_2	10	20		30
S_3		20	20	40
Demand	20	40	20	

The R and K values **2** are:

	$K_1 = 6$	$K_2 = 7$	$K_3 = -1$
$R_1 = 0$	X [6]	[4]	[0]
$R_2 = 0$	X [6]	X [7]	[0]
$R_3 = 1$	[5]	X [8]	X [0]

where X indicates an occupied cell.

The improvement indices are:

$$I_{12} = 4 - 0 - 7 = -3$$
$$I_{13} = 0 - 0 - (-1) = 1$$
$$I_{23} = 0 - 0 - (-1) = 1$$
$$I_{31} = 5 - 1 - 6 = -2$$

Since there are negative improvement indices we may improve the solution. We choose cell $(1, 2)$ to become occupied as it has the most negative improvement index. We form a loop as shown below:

X	i	
X	X	
	X	X

Adding and subtracting θ as required we have:

$10 - \theta$	θ	
$10 + \theta$	$20 - \theta$	
	20	20

We choose θ to be as large as possible, in this case $\theta = 10$. We then obtain:

	10	
20	10	
	20	20

The R and K values for this solution are:

	$K_1 = 3$	$K_2 = 4$	$K_3 = -4$
$R_1 = 0$	6	X 4	0
$R_2 = 3$	X 6	X 7	0
$R_3 = 4$	5	X 8	X 0

where X indicates an occupied cell.

The improvement indices are:

$$I_{11} = 6 - 0 - 3 = 3$$
$$I_{13} = 0 - 0 - (-4) = 4$$
$$I_{23} = 0 - 3 - (-4) = 1$$
$$I_{31} = 5 - 4 - 3 = -2$$

Again there is a negative improvement index in cell (3, 1). We form a loop as shown:

	X	
X	X	
	X	X

Adding and subtracting θ as required we have:

	10	
$20 - \theta$	$10 + \theta$	
θ	$20 - \theta$	20

We now take $\theta = 20$ and obtain:

	10	
	30	
20		20

This solution is degenerate as only four cells are occupied. In order to calculate the R and K values we need five cells occupied and so we put a zero in cell (3, 2) and regard it as occupied.
The R and K values are now:

	$K_1 = 1$	$K_2 = 4$	$K_3 = -4$
$R_1 = 0$	6	X 4	0
$R_2 = 3$	6	X 7	0
$R_3 = 4$	X 5	X 8	X 0

The improvement indices are now:

$$I_{11} = 6 - 0 - 1 = 5$$
$$I_{13} = 0 - 0 - (-4) = 4$$

$$I_{21} = 6 - 3 - 1 = 2$$
$$I_{23} = 0 - 3 - (-4) = 1$$

As all of these are non-negative this solution is optimal.

(c) Send   10 units from S_1 to D_2
                               30 units from S_2 to D_2
                               20 units from S_3 to D_1

The remaining 20 units at S_3 are not sent as they are to be sent to the dummy destination.
The cost of this pattern of transportation is:

$$(10 \times 4) + (30 \times 7) + (20 \times 5)$$
$$= 350$$

Example 4

A furniture manufacturer makes desks at its three factories at Ashford (A), Bedminster (B) and Cowplain (C). It has two retail outlets at Poolminster (P) and Ringwater (R). The number of desks available at each factory and the number required at each outlet are shown in the table below together with the costs of transporting desks between the factories and outlets.

Outlet

		P	**Q**	Available
	A	5	7	50
Factory	**B**	8	6	60
	C	9	10	90
	Demand	120	80	

The manufacturer wishes to find the cheapest distribution pattern. Formulate this as a linear programming problem, carefully defining the decision variables and explaining briefly how you obtained the constraints.

Answer

Let x_{ij} be the number of desks sent from factory i to outlet j.
The total cost of distribution is then:

$$C = 5x_{AP} + 7x_{AQ} + 8x_{BP} + 6x_{BQ} + 9x_{CP} + 10x_{CQ}$$

This is the sum of the costs on each route, which are given by:

$$(\text{number sent}) \times (\text{unit cost})$$

The objective is to minimise C.
Total number available $= 50 + 60 + 90$
                                       $= 200$
Total number required $= 120 + 80$
                                       $= 200$

The problem is balanced as these two numbers are equal. This means there will be no slack and so all the constraints will be equations rather than inequations. We have then:

factory A: $x_{AP} + x_{AQ} = 50$
factory B: $x_{BP} + x_{BQ} = 60$
factory C: $x_{CP} + x_{CQ} = 90$
outlet P: $x_{AP} + x_{BP} + x_{CP} = 120$
outlet Q: $x_{AQ} + x_{BQ} + x_{CQ} = 80$

In addition we require each of the decision variables to be non-negative.

Revision exercise 1

1 In each of the following cases write down the north-west corner solution.

(a)

	1	2	3	Available
A	5	8	9	80
B	10	6	8	50
C	7	5	6	10
Demand	40	20	80	

(b)

	1	2	3	Available
A	8	6	9	20
B	6	3	8	30
C	10	7	9	70
Demand	90	20	10	

(c)

	1	2	3	Available
A	10	7	5	15
B	12	8	6	35
C	15	9	8	20
Demand	25	15	30	

2 Find the cost of the transportation pattern you found in **1(a)**.

3 **(a)** Show that the north-west corner solution you obtained in **1(b)** is optimal and state the minimum total cost.
   (b) Obtain another transportation pattern with this same minimum total cost.

4 (a) Show that the north-west corner solution you obtained in **1(c)** is not optimal.

(b) Use the stepping-stone method to obtain a transportation pattern with minimum cost and give this minimum cost.

5 Two supermarkets, S_1 and S_2, each require 50 turkeys. Three farms, F_1, F_2 and F_3, have 25, 45 and 60 turkeys available respectively. The unit costs of transport are shown in the table below.

		Supermarket	
		S_1	S_2
	F_1	3	5
Farm	F_2	6	4
	F_3	7	7

(a) Show that the problem is unbalanced and draw a transportation tableau for the corresponding balanced problem.

(b) Write down the north-west corner solution and then use the stepping-stone method to obtain an optimal solution.

(c) Which of the farms does not distribute all its turkeys when the above optimal pattern of transportation is used?

6 A car hire company has 37 cars of the same model. On Friday afternoon 20 are at depot A, 5 are at depot B and 12 are at depot C. On the following Monday morning 10 are required at depot P, 15 at depot Q and 12 at depot R. The distances, in miles, between the depots are shown in the table below.

	P	**Q**	**R**
A	20	15	12
B	32	25	10
C	35	30	12

The manager wishes to redistribute the cars between the depots so as to cover the minimum total mileage. Obtain the minimum transportation pattern and give the total distance covered.

7 A transportation problem involves the following costs, supply and demand:

	D_1	D_2	D_3	Supply
S_1	5	2	2	7
S_2	7	3	4	5
S_3	6	4	3	3
Demand	4	5	6	

(a) Write down the north-west corner solution.

(b) Use the stepping-stone method to obtain an optimal solution and give its cost.

8 Formulate question **7** as a linear programming problem.

Test yourself	**What to review**

If your answer is incorrect:

Review Heinemann Book D2 pages 6–13, 18–19

1 Ashport Minibuses has three depots at P, Q and R and three schools wish to hire minibuses from them. On a given day there are six minibuses at P, two minibuses at Q and three minibuses at R. School 1 requires two minibuses, school 2 requires five minibuses and school 3 requires four minibuses. The distances, in miles, between the depots and the schools are shown in the table below.

		School		
		1	**2**	**3**
Depot	**P**	5	4	7
	Q	6	2	5
	R	7	9	4

The manager of Ashport Minibuses wishes to distribute the minibuses to the schools so that the total distance travelled is as small as possible.

	1	**2**	**3**
P	2	x	
Q		y	z
R			3

The above table shows a possible transportation pattern.

(a) Find the values of x, y and z.

(b) Find the cost of this pattern using the values of x, y and z found in **(a)**.

(c) By finding improvement indices, show that this pattern has minimum total cost.

(d) Obtain another transportation pattern that has the same minimum total cost.

2 A farmer has two farms at Ambridge and Bridgemoor. Ambridge has 260 sacks of potatoes available and Bridgemoor has 140 sacks of potatoes available. Three supermarkets at Midport, Nextbridge and Oxville require 180 sacks, 120 sacks and 200 sacks of potatoes respectively. The costs in £s of transporting a sack of potatoes from the farms to the supermarkets are shown in the table below.

Review Heinemann Book D2 pages 16–18, 20–22

Supermarket

		M	N	O
Farm	A	10	6	11
	B	12	8	10

(a) Show that not all the supermarkets are going to receive the potatoes they require.

(b) Use the north-west corner rule to obtain an initial basic feasible solution and then use the stepping-stone method to obtain a distribution pattern that has total minimum cost.

(c) State this transportation pattern and give its cost. Which supermarkets will not receive their full requirements? How many sacks will each receive?

Test yourself answers

1 (a) $x = 4, y = 1, z = 1$ (b) 45
   (c) $I_{13} = 0$ (d)
   $I_{21} = 3$
   $I_{31} = 5$
   $I_{32} = 8$

2	3	1
	2	
		3

2 (a) Number required $= 180 + 120 + 200 = 500$
   Number available $= 260 + 140 = 400$
   $500 - 400 = 100$

(b) Initial solution

	M	N	O
A	180	80	
B		40	100
Dummy			100

Optimal solution

	M	N	O
A	140	120	
B			140
Dummy	40		60

(c) cost $= 3520$
   M and O do not get what they require.
   M gets 140 sacks.
   N gets 120 sacks.
   O gets 140 sacks.

Allocation (assignment) problems

2

Key points to remember

1 The Hungarian algorithm

Step 1 Find the opportunity cost matrix.
Step 2 Test for an optimal assignment. If an optimal assignment can be made, make it and stop.
Step 3 Revise the opportunity cost matrix and return to step 2.

2 Testing for an optimal assignment

If the minimum number of straight lines (vertical and horizontal) required to cover all the zeros, in the opportunity cost matrix, is equal to the number of rows and columns in the matrix then an assignment can be made.

3 Revising the opportunity cost matrix

To revise the opportunity cost matrix:
(i) **subtract** the smallest number not covered by a line from all numbers not covered by a straight line
(ii) **add** this number to every number (including zeros) lying at the intersection of any two lines.

Example 1

ABC taxis has four taxis, 1, 2, 3 and 4, and there are four customers, P, Q, R and S requiring taxis. The distances between the taxis and the customers are given in the table below, in miles. The company wishes to assign the taxis to customers so that the total distance travelled is a minimum.

		Customers			
		P	**Q**	**R**	**S**
	1	10	8	4	6
Taxis	**2**	6	4	12	8
	3	14	10	8	2
	4	4	14	10	8

(a) Obtain the opportunity cost matrix.

(b) Obtain an optimal assignment and give the minimum total distance.

Answer

(a) The row minima are 4, 4, 2 and 4.

After carrying out row reduction we obtain

6	4	0	2
2	0	8	4
12	8	6	0
0	10	6	4

Since all the column minima are zero, column reduction produces no change. The above is therefore the opportunity cost matrix.

(b) The minimum number of lines required to cover the zeros is four:

6	4	0*	2
2	0*	8	4
12	8	6	0*
0*	10	6	4

We can therefore make an optimal assignment. Since there is only one zero in each row this must be used. The optimal assignment is therefore:

$$1 \rightarrow R \qquad \text{distance 4}$$
$$2 \rightarrow Q \qquad \text{distance 4}$$
$$3 \rightarrow S \qquad \text{distance 2}$$
$$4 \rightarrow P \qquad \text{distance 4}$$

Minimum distance = 14 miles

Example 2

A department manager has four jobs that she wishes to assign to four workers. The estimated costs of assigning a particular worker to a particular job are shown in the table below.

	1	2	3	4
Andrew	80	40	50	46
Barbara	40	70	20	25
Coral	30	10	20	30
David	35	20	25	30

The assignment is to be made so that the total cost is a minimum. Use the Hungarian algorithm to obtain an optimal assignment and find its cost.

Answer

The row minima are 40, 20, 10 and 20.
After carrying out row reduction we obtain

40	0	10	6
20	50	0	5
20	0	10	20
15	0	5	10

The column minima are 15, 0, 0 and 5.
After carrying out column reduction we obtain the following opportunity cost matrix:

25	0	10	1
5	50	0	0
5	0	10	15
0	0	5	5

The zeros may be covered by three lines:

25	0	10	1
5	50	0	0
5	0	10	15
0	0	5	5

Since 3 is less than 4, the number of row and columns, we must now revise the opportunity cost matrix.
The smallest uncovered number is 1 so we subtract 1 from each of the six uncovered numbers and add 1 to the two numbers that lie at the intersection of the lines:

24	0	9	0
5	51	0	0
4	0	9	14
0	1	5	5

The minimum number of lines required to cover the zeros is now four:

24	0	9	0*
5	51	0*	0
4	0*	9	14
0*	1	5	5

An optimal assignment can now be made. As there is only one zero in column 1 and column 3 they must be used. Also, as there is only one zero in row 3 this must be used. This implies that we must use the zero in cell (1, 4).

The optimal assignment is then:

$$A \rightarrow 4 \qquad \text{cost } 46$$
$$B \rightarrow 3 \qquad \text{cost } 20$$
$$C \rightarrow 2 \qquad \text{cost } 10$$
$$D \rightarrow 1 \qquad \text{cost } 35$$

Total minimum cost = 111

Example 3

A head of department has four teachers to assign to pure maths (1), mechanics (2), statistics (3) and decision maths (4). All of the teachers have taught the courses in the past and have been evaluated with a score from 0 to 100. The scores are shown in the table below.

	1	2	3	4
Peters	80	55	45	45
Richards	58	35	70	50
Thomas	70	50	80	65
White	90	70	40	80

The head of department wishes to know the optimal assignment of teachers to courses that will maximise the overall total score. Use the Hungarian algorithm to solve this problem.

Answer

Since this is a maximising problem we first produce a cost matrix by subtracting each entry from 100. We obtain:

	1	2	3	4	Row minimum
P	20	45	55	55	20
R	42	65	30	50	30
T	30	50	20	35	20
W	10	30	60	20	10

Reducing the rows we obtain:

	0	25	35	35
	12	35	0	20
	10	30	0	15
	0	20	50	10
Column minimum	0	20	0	10

Reducing the columns gives:

0	5	35	25
12	15	0	10
10	10	0	5
0	0	50	0

We may cover the zeros with three lines:

0	5	35	25
12	15	0	10
10	10	0	5
0	0	50	0

(There are other ways of drawing in the three lines. These would lead through different configurations to the same optimal solution.)

The smallest uncovered number is 5. Adding and subtracting as required by the algorithm we obtain:

0	5	40	25
7	10	0	5
5	5	0	0
0	0	55	0

Four lines are now required to cover all the zeros:

0*	5	40	25
7	10	0*	5
5	5	0	0*
0	0*	55	0

An optimal assignment can now be made.

There is only one zero in row 1 (1, 1) so we use it.
There is only one zero in row 2 (2, 3) so we use it.
There is only one zero in column 2 (4, 2) so we use it.

To complete the allocation we must use cell (3, 4). Returning to the original data we have:

$$P \rightarrow 1 \qquad \text{score } 80$$
$$R \rightarrow 3 \qquad \text{score } 70$$
$$T \rightarrow 4 \qquad \text{score } 65$$
$$W \rightarrow 2 \qquad \text{score } 70$$

Total maximum score $= 285$

Example 4

A market research company has three clients, A, B and C, who wish them to conduct a sample survey. Four researchers are available but each can only handle one client. The table below shows the number of hours required for each researcher to complete each job.

Job

	A	B	C
1	150	210	270
2	175	240	220
3	180	230	225
4	160	240	240

Researcher

Determine which researcher should be assigned to each job to keep the total time involved to a minimum. Which researcher does not get a job?

Answer

Since the number of researchers exceeds the number of jobs by 1 we add a dummy job D and then use the Hungarian algorithm to solve the resulting problem.

	A	B	C	D
1	150	210	270	0
2	175	240	220	0
3	180	230	225	0
4	160	240	240	0

Row reduction produces no change as each row contains a zero. The column minima are 150, 210, 220 and 0 respectively.

Reducing the columns we obtain:

0	0	50	0
25	30	0	0
30	20	5	0
10	30	20	0

The zeros may be covered by three lines so no assignment is possible.

The smallest uncovered number is 5. Adding and subtracting this number in accordance with the algorithm gives:

0	0	50	5
25	30	0	5
25	15	0	0
5	25	15	0

Again the zeros may be covered by three lines. The smallest uncovered number is 5. Adding and subtracting this number in accordance with the algorithm gives:

0	0*	55	10
20	25	0*	5
20	10	0	0*
0*	20	15	0

The minimum number of lines now required to cover the zeros is four, so we can now make an optimal assignment.
There is only one zero in column 2, (1, 2) so we must use it.
There is only one zero in row 2 (2, 3) so we must use it. We cannot then use (3, 3) so we must use (3, 4).

Consequently we must use (4, 1) in row 4:

$$
\begin{array}{lll}
1 \rightarrow B & \text{time 210} \\
2 \rightarrow C & \text{time 220} \\
3 \rightarrow D & \text{time 0} \\
4 \rightarrow A & \text{time 160}
\end{array}
$$

Total minimum time = 590 hours

Researcher 3 does not get a job as he is assigned to the dummy job D.

Revision exercise 2

1 Three accountants, Peter, Rita and Susan, are to be assigned to three projects, 1, 2 and 3. The assignment costs in units of £1000 are shown in the table below.

		Project	
	1	**2**	**3**
P	15	9	12
R	7	5	10
S	13	4	6

Accountant

Find the assignment that minimises the total cost. Give this minimum total cost.

2 Four precision components are to be shaped using four machine tools, one tool being assigned to each component. The machining times, in minutes, are given the table below.

	Component			
	1	**2**	**3**	**4**
A	21	20	39	36
B	25	22	24	25
C	36	22	36	26
D	34	21	25	39

Machine tool

Determine how the machine tools should be assigned so that the total machining time will be as small as possible. State the minimum time.

3 A department store has leased a new store and wishes to decide how to place four departments in four locations so as to maximise total profits. The table below give the profits, in £1000, when the departments are allocated to the various locations.

	Location			
	1	**2**	**3**	**4**
Shoes	20	16	22	18
Toys	25	28	15	21
Auto	27	20	23	26
Housewares	24	22	23	22

Department

Find the assignment that maximises total profits.

4 Bill and Jane have four jobs, A, B, C and D, they need to have done in their new home. They get estimates from four general builders for these jobs. These are shown, in £, in the table below.

Job

Builder		A	B	C	D
	1	280	200	290	210
	2	220	230	260	240
	3	270	280	310	250
	4	290	210	340	200

Bill and Jane wish to allocate the jobs to the builders so that the total cost is a minimum. Find two allocations of jobs to builders that have the minimum total cost. State this cost.

5 Four machine operators are available to perform three jobs. The time taken, in hours, by each operator to carry out each job is shown in the table below.

Job

Operator		1	2	3
	A	51	42	29
	B	44	39	38
	C	33	45	42
	D	34	47	46

The manager wishes to allocate the operators to jobs so that the total time taken is a minimum. Obtain an allocation of operators to jobs that involves a minimum time. Give this minimum time. Which operator does not get a job?

6 Formulate the assignment problem given in question **1** as a linear programming problem.

| Test yourself | What to review |

If your answer is incorrect:

1 Each summer a firm employs four students to help cover for holiday absences. This year Ali, Brenda, Carl and Deborah have been given jobs and need to be trained before starting work. Bearing in mind the previous experience of the students, the manager assesses the likely training costs, in £, to be as given in the table below.

Review Heinemann Book D2 pages 32–38

	Driver (**1**)	Packer (**2**)	Accounts clerk (**3**)	Computer operator (**4**)
Ali	85	90	120	70
Brenda	130	125	120	100
Carl	115	120	100	115
Deborah	160	150	135	125

Use the Hungarian algorithm to obtain the assignment of students to jobs which minimises the overall cost of training.

2 The head of a college's business department has decided to use the Hungarian algorithm to assign lecturers to courses next year. As a criterion for judging who should teach which course the head reviews the past three years' teaching evaluations and records a rating for each lecturer for each course. These ratings are shown in the table below.

Review Heinemann Book D2 pages 43–44

	Statistics	**Management**	**Finance**	**Economics**
Green	87	94	76	72
Peach	74	92	85	69
Rust	86	70	80	76
White	71	87	89	92

Find the best assignment of lecturers to courses to maximise the overall teaching rating.

Test yourself answers

1 Ali → driver   85
Brenda → computer operator   100
Carl → accounts clerk   100
Deborah → packer   150

or   Ali → driver   85
     Brenda → packer   125
     Carl → accounts clerk   100
     Deborah → computer operator   125

Total minimum cost = £435

2 Green → management   94
Peach → finance   85
Rust → statistics   86
White → economics   92

Overall teaching rating = 357

The travelling salesman problem

3

Example 1

A company director wishes to visit his five offices situated in Ansty (A), Birdtown (B), Coalmouth (C), Downborough (D) and Edenville (E). The diagram below shows the roads between these offices and the distances, in km.

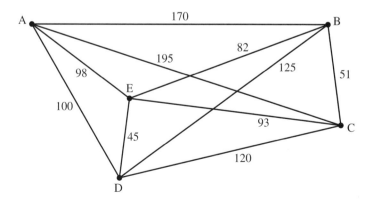

The company director lives in town A and wishes to start and finish his journey there. He wishes to find a route that will visit each of his offices and involve him travelling a minimum distance.

(a) Use Kruskal's algorithm to obtain a minimum spanning tree. State the order in which edges are selected.

(b) (i) Hence determine an initial upper bound for the length of the route planned.
(ii) Starting from your initial upper bound and using shortcuts obtain a route that is less than 515 km.

(c) (i) Use the nearest neighbour algorithm, starting at A, to obtain an upper bound for the optimal tour.
(ii) Can you obtain a shorter tour by using the algorithm and starting at some other vertex? If so, obtain such a tour and give its length.

Answer

(a) The shortest edge is ED (45), so select it:

The next shortest edge is BC (51), so select it:

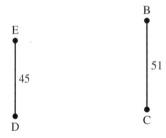

The shortest remaining edge is BE (82), so select it as it does not create a cycle:

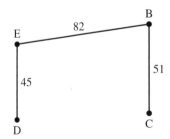

The next shortest edge is EC (93) but it cannot be chosen as it creates a cycle with edges already selected.

The shortest remaining edge is AE (98) and this can be chosen as it does not create a cycle. We have now selected four edges and so we have a minimum spanning tree:

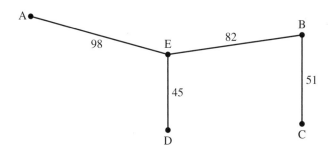

The edges were selected in the order:

$$ED, BC, BE \text{ and } AE$$

The weight of this minimum spanning tree is:

$$45 + 51 + 82 + 98 = 276 \, km$$

(b) (i)   An initial upper bound is:

$$2 \times \text{(weight of a minimum spanning tree)}$$
$$= 2 \times 276 = 552 \, km$$

The route is shown below as a dotted line:

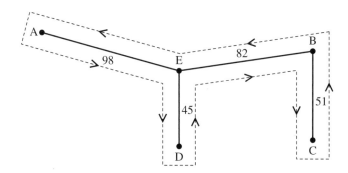

(ii) For example, if, when we reach C, we return directly to A we save:

$$(98 + 82 + 51) - AC \, (195)$$
$$= 231 - 195$$
$$= 36 \, km$$

If we also replace DEB by DB we save:

$$45 + 82 - DB \, (125)$$
$$= 127 - 125$$
$$= 2$$

Total saving, using these two shortcuts, is $36 + 2 = 38$.
We then have a route AEDBCA of length $552 - 38 = 514 \, km$.

(c) **(i)** Starting at A the nearest vertex is E (AE = 98).

The nearest vertex to E is D (ED = 45).

The nearest vertex to D is (DC =120).

The nearest vertex to C is B (CB = 51).

To complete the tour we must now use BA (170).

The tour is then AEDCBA, of length

$$98 + 45 + 120 + 51 + 170 = 484 \, \text{km}$$

(ii) A shorter tour can be obtained. Since no edge incident at E has length greater than 100 we start there. The nearest neighbour algorithm gives:

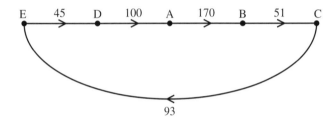

The length of this tour **EDABCE** is:

$$45 + 100 + 170 + 51 + 93 = 459 \, \text{km}$$

(Starting at B we also get a tour of length 459 km, namely BCEDAB.)

Example 2

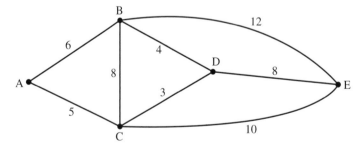

(a) For the above network draw up a table in which the entries are the shortest distances between pairs of vertices.

(b) Use the nearest neighbour algorithm, starting at A, to obtain a tour in the transformed network. Give its length and interpret the tour in terms of the original network.

(c) Use the nearest neighbour algorithm, starting at different vertices, to obtain tours that have a shorter length. Interpret these tours in terms of the original network.

Answer

(a)

	A	B	C	D	E
A	—	6	5	8	15
B	6	—	7	4	12
C	5	7	—	3	10
D	8	4	3	—	8
E	15	12	10	8	—

The shortest route from A to D is ACD (length 8).
The shortest route from A to E is ACE (length 15).
The shortest route from B to C is BD (length 7).

(b) From the table, starting at A:

    nearest vertex to A is C (AC = 5)
    nearest vertex to C is D (CD = 3)
    nearest vertex to D is B (DB = 4)
    nearest vertex to B is E (BE = 12)

We could show the above on the distance matrix as:

	A	B	C	D	E
A	—	6	5	8	15
B	6	—	7	④	12
C	⑤	7	—	3	10
D	8	4	③	—	8
E	15	⑫	10	8	—

We complete the tour by using EA, of length 15. The tour is
ACDBEA:

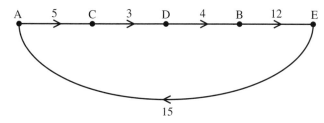

Total length = 39.

Since EA is not in the original network, we must replace it by ECA.
(All the other edges used are in the original network.) The tour is
then ACDBECA.

Vertex C is visited twice on this tour.

(c) **(i)** Starting at B we obtain:

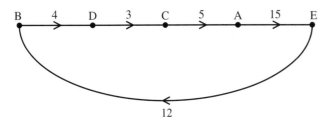

This is the tour above in reverse and has length 39. The tour in the original network is BDCACEB.

(ii) Starting at C we obtain:

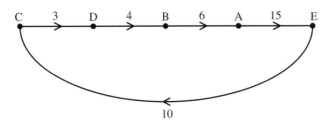

The tour is CDBAEC, of length 38.
The tour in the original network is CDBACEC.

(iii) Starting at D we obtain:

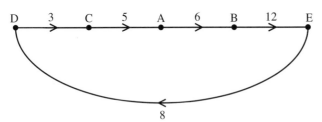

The tour is DCABED, of length 34.
The tour in the original network is also DCABED.

(iv) Starting at E we obtain:

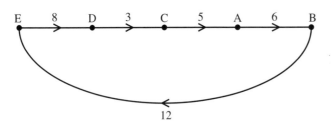

The tour is EDCABE (the reverse of (iii)), of length 34. The tour in the original network is also EDCABE.

Example 3
Angela (A) has four brothers, Ben (B), Charles (C), Darren (D) and Edward (E). She wishes to visit each of them once, to deliver Christmas presents, and then return home. She wishes to cover a

minimum distance in doing this. The distances, in miles, between the homes of A, B, C, D and E are shown in the table below.

	A	B	C	D	E
A	—	10	25	15	18
B	10	—	16	8	14
C	25	16	—	10	14
D	15	8	10	—	7
E	18	14	14	7	—

(a) Find a minimum spanning tree that connects the five homes.
(b) Hence find an initial upper bound for the total distance Angela travels.
(c) Improve your upper bound by making shortcuts.
(d) By deleting vertex D find a lower bound.

Answer

(a)

	1	2	5	3	4
	A	B	C	D	E
A	—	10	25	15	18
B	-⑩	—	16	8	14
C	25	16	—	⑩	14
D	15	⑧	10	—	7
E	18	14	14	⑦	—

Carrying out Prim's algorithm as shown in the above table we obtain the following minimum spanning tree:

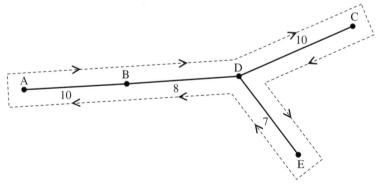

(b) The initial upper bound is:

$$2 \times (\text{weight of minimum spanning tree})$$
$$= 2 \times (10 + 8 + 10 + 7) = 70 \text{ miles}$$

This corresponds to the route shown by $-\!\!\rightarrow\!\!-$ in the figure above.

(c) (i) For example, if we replace CDE by CE we save $(10 + 7) - 14 = 3$ miles.

(ii) For example, if we replace EDBA by EA we save $(7 + 8 + 10) - 18 = 7$ miles.

The route ABDCEA then has length $70 - 3 - 7 = 60$ miles.

An improved upper bound is then 60 miles.

(d) If we remove D and all edges incident to D we obtain the distance matrix:

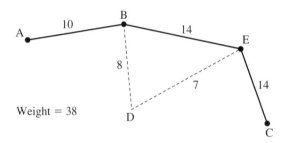

	1	2	4	3
	A	**B**	**C**	**E**
A	——	10	25	18
B	10	——	16	14
C	25	16	——	14
E	18	14	14	——

Carrying out Prim's algorithm as shown above we obtain the minimum spanning tree:

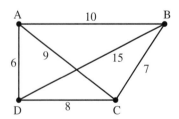

Weight = 38

The two shortest edges at D are DB (8) and DE (7).

Hence a lower bound is:

(weight of minimum spanning tree found above) $+ 8 + 7$

$= 38 + 15 = 53$ miles

Revision exercise 3

1

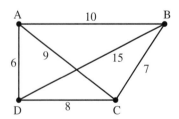

(a) Find a minimum spanning tree for the above network and hence find an initial upper bound for the total length of the solution of the travelling salesman problem.

(b) Obtain a better upper bound by using a shortcut.

2

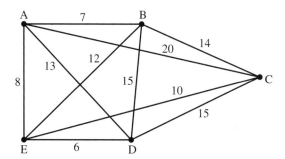

(a) Find a minimum spanning tree for the above network and hence find an initial upper bound for the total length of the solution of the travelling salesman problem.

(b) Obtain a better upper bound by using a shortcut.

3

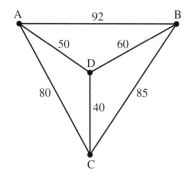

(a) Find a minimum spanning tree for the above network and hence find an initial upper bound for the total length of the solution of the travelling salesman problem.

(b) By using shortcuts find an upper bound less than 270.

4 For each of the networks in questions **1**, **2** and **3**:

(a) obtain a lower bound by removing A

(b) by removing a different vertex obtain a better lower bound.

5 For each of the networks in questions **1**, **2** and **3** obtain an upper bound by using the nearest neighbour algorithm starting at A.

6 For the network given in question **2** obtain a better upper bound using the nearest neighbour algorithm and starting at a vertex other than A.

7

	A	**B**	**C**	**D**	**E**
A	—	85	90	60	80
B	85	—	135	130	145
C	90	135	—	60	160
D	60	130	60	—	115
E	80	145	160	115	—

The above table shows the distances, in miles, between some cities. A commercial traveller, Sue, has to visit each city once, starting and finishing at A. She wishes to minimise her total travelling distance.

(a) Find a minimum spanning tree for the network.

(b) Hence find an initial upper bound for Sue's problem.

(c) Reduce this upper bound to a value below 480 miles by using shortcuts.

(d) Obtain a lower bound by removing vertex A.

(e) Use your answers to **(c)** and **(d)** to write down an inequality satisfied by the optimal length of the tour.

(f) State a tour that satisfies the inequality found in **(e)**.

8

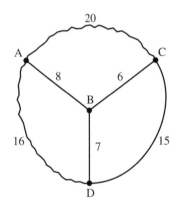

The network above shows four locations in a park and the tracks connecting them. The numbers on the edges are the distances in km.

(a) Draw a network showing the shortest distances between the locations.

(b) Use the nearest neighbour algorithm on the network drawn in **(a)** to obtain an upper bound to the length of an optimal tour in this network that starts at A.

(c) Interpret your result for **(b)** in terms of the original network.

9

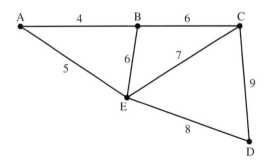

(a) For the network opposite, draw up a table in which the entries are the shortest distances between pairs of vertices.

(b) Use the nearest neighbour algorithm on this table to obtain an upper bound to the length of the tour in the complete network, which starts and finishes at A and visits every vertex exactly once. Interpret your result in terms of the original network.

(c) Find a better tour starting at a vertex other than A.

Test yourself	What to review

If your answer is incorrect:

1 A delivery driver, Tom, is based at warehouse W and needs to deliver goods to shops at A, B C, D and E. The distances between the various places, in miles, are given in the table below. Tom wishes to visit each shop once and return to W, covering a minimum distance.

Review Heinemann Book D2 pages 47–54, 57–62

	W	**A**	**B**	**C**	**D**	**E**
W	—	110	50	52	84	65
A	110	—	84	120	35	97
B	50	84	—	103	55	100
C	52	120	103	—	137	47
D	84	35	55	137	—	102
E	65	97	100	47	102	—

(a) Starting from W, use Prim's algorithm to find a minimum spanning tree for the network that models the above data.

(b) (i) Hence find an initial upper bound for the distance travelled by Tom.
(ii) Use a shortcut to reduce the upper bound to a value below 340.

(c) By deleting W and all edges incident to W, find a lower bound to the distance travelled by Tom.

(d) Use your answers to **(b)** and **(c)** to make a comment on the length of Tom's optimal tour.

(e) Draw a diagram to show Tom's optimal tour.

2

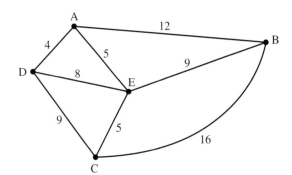

*Review Heinemann Book D2
pages 66–72*

The network above shows a number of villages and the roads connecting them. The distances are given in kilometres.
(a) Draw a complete network showing the shortest distances between the villages. (This may be done by inspection. The application of an algorithm is not required.)
(b) Use the nearest neighbour algorithm on the complete network to obtain an upper bound to the length of a tour in this network which starts and finishes at A and visits each village exactly once.
(c) Interpret your result in **(b)** in terms of the original network. Which village is visited more than once?
(d) Using the nearest neighbour algorithm and starting at a vertex other than A show that it is possible to obtain an upper bound less than 40. Give this route.

Test yourself answers

1 (a)

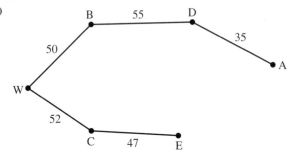

(b) (i) Initial upper bound $= 2(50 + 55 + 35 + 52 + 47) = 2(239) = 478$ miles
 (ii) Use AE instead of ADBWCE saving $(35 + 55 + 50 + 52 + 47) - 97 = 239 - 97 = 142$ miles
  New upper bound $= 478 - 142 = 336$ miles
(c) Minimum spanning tree when W is removed

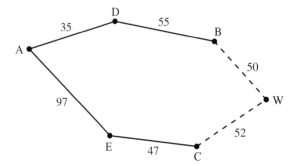

The two shortest edges at W are WB (50) and WC (52), so a lower bound is

$$35 + 50 + 55 + 97 + 47 + 52 = 336$$

(d) The length L of the optimal route must satisfy $336 \leqslant L \leqslant 336$, so $L = 336$
(e) Optimal route from C is then:

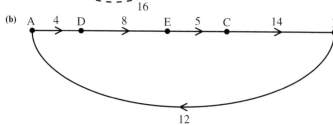

2 (a)

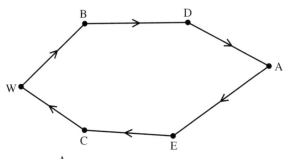

(b)

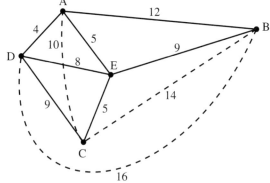

Upper bound = 43 km

Tour = ADECBA

(c) In the original network the optimal tour is ADECEBA
E is visited twice.

(d)

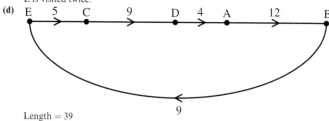

Length = 39
or BECDAB, also of length 39

Game theory

4

Key points to remember

1 A **two person game** is one in which only two parties can play.

2 A **zero-sum game** is one in which the sum of the losses for one player is equal to the sum of the gains for the other player.

3 A two person zero-sum game for which max over all rows (row minimum) = min over all columns (column maximum) is said to have a **saddle point**. The common value of both sides of the above equation is the **value** v of the game to the row player.

4 **Dominance rule for rows**
If every entry in a given row R_1 is **less than or equal to** the corresponding entry in another given row R_2, then R_1 is said to be **dominated** by R_2 and may therefore be eliminated.

5 **Dominance rule for columns**
If every entry in a given column C_1 is **greater than or equal to** the corresponding entry in another given column C_2, then C_1 is said to be **dominated** by C_2 and may therefore be eliminated.

6 To solve a two person zero-sum game:
Step 1 Check to see if the game has a saddle point. If not go to step 2.
Step 2 Eliminate as many rows and columns as possible using the principle of dominance.
Step 3 Solve the resulting game by an appropriate method.

Example 1
Show that the two person zero-sum game with payoff matrix:

$$A\begin{array}{c} \\ \\ \\ \end{array}\overset{B}{\begin{pmatrix} -1 & 1 \\ 3 & 5 \\ 7 & 8 \end{pmatrix}}$$

has a saddle point. State the strategies for the two players and give the value of the game.

Answer

The row minima are -1, 3 and 7 respectively.
The maximum of the row minima is therefore 7.
The column maxima are 7 and 8 respectively.
The minimum of the column maxima is therefore 7.

Since maximum of row minima = minimum of column maxima = 7, the game has a saddle point, using **3**.
Player A should play strategy 3 and player B should play strategy 1.
The value of the game is 7 to player A.

Example 2

Two players, Alan and Betty, play a zero-sum game. Alan has two possible strategies A_1 and A_2 and Betty has three possible strategies B_1, B_2 and B_3. The payoff matrix for the game is:

		B		
		B_1	B_2	B_3
A	A_1	7	-1	6
	A_2	2	8	3

(a) Find Alan's and Betty's play safe strategies.
(b) If they know in advance that the other player will play safe, determine which strategies Alan and Betty will play.

Answer

(a) The row minima are -1 and 2 and so if Alan is playing safe he will play strategy A_2 since $2 > -1$.

The column maxima are 7, 8 and 6. If Betty is playing safe she will play strategy B_3 since 6 is the smallest of these. Alan will gain 3 and Betty will lose 3.
(b) If Alan knows Betty is playing safe, i.e. is playing B_3, then Alan will switch to A_1 since $6 > 3$ and his gain will be 6. If Betty knows Alan is playing safe, i.e. is playing A_2, then Betty will switch to B_1 since $2 < 3$ and her loss will be 2.

Example 3

Apply the principle of dominance to each of the following payoff matrices:

(a)

		B		
		I	II	III
	I	3	5	1
A	II	5	7	8
	III	10	1	4

(b)

		B	
		I	II
	I	5	8
A	II	7	2
	III	3	6

(c)

		B		
		I	**II**	**III**
	I	1	−1	3
A	**II**	1	5	4
	III	3	2	5

Answer

(a) A_1 is dominated by A_2 since $5 > 3, 7 > 5$ and $8 > 1$, so we have:

5	7	8
10	1	4

using **4**

B_3 is dominated by B_2 since $7 < 8$ and $1 < 4$, so we have:

5	7
10	1

using **5**

(b) A_3 is dominated by A_1 since $5 > 3$ and $8 > 6$, so we have:

5	8
7	2

using **4**

(c) A_1 is dominated by A_2 since $1 = 1, 5 > -1$ and $4 > 3$, so we have:

1	5	4
3	2	5

using **4**

B_3 is dominated by B_1 since $1 < 4$ and $3 < 5$, so we have:

1	3
3	2

using **5**

Example 4

		Y	
		Y_1	**Y_2**
X	**X_1**	−1	8
	X_2	7	1

For the payoff matrix above find:
(a) the optimal mixed strategies for both players
(b) the value of the game.

Answer

Suppose X plays strategy X_1 a fraction p of the time and strategy X_2 a fraction $(1 - p)$ of the time. Then the gain for X if Y plays strategy Y_1 is:

$$-p + 7(1 - p) = 7 - 8p$$

the gain for X if Y plays strategy Y_2 is:

$$8p + (1 - p) = 1 + 7p$$

If v is the value of the game then we need to find p so as to maximise v where $v \leqslant 7 - 8p$ and $v \leqslant 1 + 7p$.

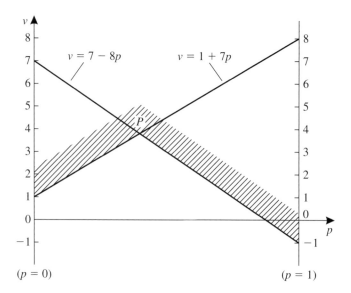

From the figure above we can see that the maximum value of v occurs at the point P where the two lines cross, P is therefore given by:

$$7 - 8p = 1 + 7p$$

$$6 = 15p$$

$$\Rightarrow p = \tfrac{6}{15} = \tfrac{2}{5}$$

and $$(1 - p) = \tfrac{3}{5}$$

X should therefore use strategy X_1 for $\tfrac{2}{5}$ of the time and strategy X_2 for $\tfrac{3}{5}$ of the time. The value of the game is given by:

$$1 + 7p \text{ when } p = \tfrac{2}{5}$$

So $v = 3\tfrac{4}{5}$

Suppose Y plays strategy Y_1 for a fraction q of the time and strategy Y_2 for a fraction $(1 - q)$ of the time. Proceeding as above, q is determined from:

$$-q + 8(1 - q) = 7q + (1 - q)$$

or
$$8 - 9q = 1 + 6q$$

$$7 = 15q$$

So
$$q = \tfrac{7}{15} \text{ and } (1 - q) = \tfrac{8}{15}$$

So Y should use strategy Y_1 for $\tfrac{7}{15}$ of the time and strategy Y_2 for $\tfrac{8}{15}$ of the time. The value of the game is:

$$1 + 6q \text{ when } q = \tfrac{7}{15}$$

So $v = 3\tfrac{4}{5}$ (as found above).

Example 5

Find the optimal mixed strategies for both players when the payoff matrix is:

Q

	Q_1	Q_2	Q_3
P_1	7	9	12
P_2	13	5	4

P

Answer

Suppose P uses strategy P_1 for a fraction p of the time and strategy P_2 for a fraction $(1 - p)$ of the time.
Then her expected gain, if Q plays Q_1, is:

$$7p + 13(1 - p) = 13 - 6p$$

Her expected gain if Q plays Q_2 is:

$$9p + 5(1 - p) = 5 + 4p$$

Her expected gain if Q plays Q_3 is:

$$12p + 4(1 - p) = 4 + 8p$$

So P wishes to maximise the game value v subject to:

$$v \leqslant 13 - 6p$$
$$v \leqslant 5 + 4p$$
$$v \leqslant 4 + 8p$$

by an appropriate choice of p.

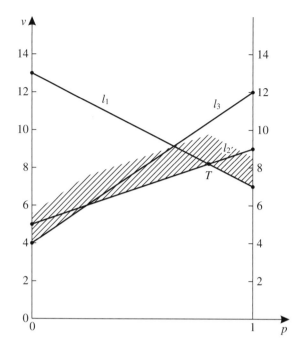

The figure above shows the lines l_1; $v = 13 - 6p$

$$l_2; \ v = 5 + 4p$$
$$l_3; \ v = 4 + 8p$$

Hence P can maximise the value of the game by choosing the value of p corresponding to the highest point T of the unshaded region. T is at the intersection of l_1 and l_2, so the value of p is given by:

$$13 - 6p = 4p + 5$$

or $$8 = 10p$$

So $$p = \tfrac{4}{5} \text{ and } (1 - p) = \tfrac{1}{5}$$

and the value of the game is $5 + 4p$ when $p = \tfrac{4}{5}$, that is $v = 8\tfrac{1}{5}$.
P should use strategy P_1 for $\tfrac{4}{5}$ of the time and strategy P_2 for $\tfrac{1}{5}$ of the time.
We also see that Q must only use strategies Q_1 and Q_2, corresponding to lines l_1 and l_2, and never Q_3.
Suppose Q uses strategy Q_1 for a fraction q of the time and strategy Q_2 for a fraction $(1 - q)$ of the time.
Then using:

$$(\text{gain for Q if P uses } P_1) = (\text{gain for Q if P uses } P_2)$$
$$7q + 9(1 - q) = 13q + 5(1 - q)$$

or $$9 - 2q = 5 + 8q$$
$$4 = 10q$$

So $$q = \tfrac{2}{5} \text{ and } (1 - q) = \tfrac{3}{5}$$

Hence Q should use Q_1 for $\tfrac{2}{5}$ of time and Q_2 for $\tfrac{3}{5}$ of time and never Q_3.

Example 6

The payoff matrix for a two person zero-sum game is:

		N	
		N_1	N_2
M	M_1	9	-3
	M_2	8	7
	M_3	6	9

Find the optimal mixed strategies for both players and the value of the game.

Answer

Since N has only two possible strategies we consider N first.
Suppose N uses strategy N_1 for a fraction p of the time and strategy N_2 for a fraction $(1 - p)$ of the time.
Then his expected loss if M plays M_1 is:

$$9p - 3(1 - p) = -3 + 12p$$

His expected loss if M plays M_2 is:

$$8p + 7(1 - p) = 7 + p$$

His expected loss if M plays M_3 is:

$$6p + 9(1 - p) = 9 - 3p$$

So N's problem is to keep his loss as small as possible. If v is the value of the game to M we require v to be as small as possible subject to:

$$v \geqslant -3 + 12p$$
$$v \geqslant 7 + p$$
$$v \geqslant 9 - 3p$$

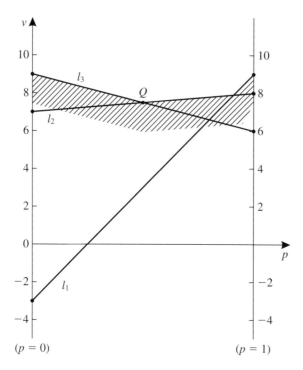

$(p = 0)$ $(p = 1)$

The inequalities are satisfied in the unshaded region and the point Q gives the required value of p. This is the intersection of the lines l_2 and l_3,

So
$$7 + p = 9 - 3p$$

or
$$4p = 2$$

So
$$p = \tfrac{1}{2} \text{ and } (1 - p) = \tfrac{1}{2}$$

and v, the value of the game, is $7 + p$ when $p = \tfrac{1}{2}$, that is $7\tfrac{1}{2}$.

So N should play both N_1 and N_2 for $\tfrac{1}{2}$ of the time.

Since the above solution occurred at the intersection of lines l_2 and l_3, strategy M_1 will not be used by M.

Suppose M uses M_2 a fraction q of the time and M_3 a fraction $(1 - q)$ of the time.
Then using:

$$\text{(gain for M if N uses } N_1) = \text{(gain for M if N uses } N_2)$$
$$8q + 6(1 - q) = 7q + 9(1 - q)$$
$$6 + 2q = 9 - 2q$$

or
$$4q = 3$$

So
$$q = \tfrac{3}{4} \text{ and } (1 - q) = \tfrac{1}{4}$$

M should therefore use strategy M_2 for a fraction $\tfrac{3}{4}$ of the time, M_3 for a fraction $\tfrac{1}{4}$ of the time and never use M_1.

Example 7

	B	
	I	**II**
A **I**	6	2
A **II**	1	5

For the payoff matrix given above:

(a) obtain the linear programming problem that when solved will give the optimal strategy for **B**

(b) solve the linear programming problem using the simplex method to obtain B's optimal strategy and the value of the game

(c) deduce the optimal strategy for A.

Answer

We first note that all entries are positive.

(a) Suppose B chooses strategy B_1 with probability p_1 and strategy B_2 with probability p_2. Then:

$$p_1 + p_2 = 1 \qquad (1)$$

If A plays strategy A_1, then the expected loss sustained by B is $6p_1 + 2p_2$. If the value of the game is v then:

$$6p_1 + 2p_2 \leqslant v \qquad (2)$$

Similarly, if A plays strategy A_2 then the expected loss sustained by B is $p_1 + 5p_2$ and so:

$$p_1 + 5p_2 \leqslant v \qquad (3)$$

B wishes to minimise v as this is A's gain. Defining $x_1 = \dfrac{p_1}{v}$ and $x_2 = \dfrac{p_2}{v}$, equation (1) becomes:

$$x_1 + x_2 = \frac{1}{v}$$

As the aim is to minimise v the objective becomes

maximise $\qquad\qquad P = x_1 + x_2$

The constraints are now:

$$6x_1 + 2x_2 \leqslant 1$$
$$x_1 + 5x_2 \leqslant 1$$

and since $p_1 \geqslant 0$ and $p_2 \geqslant 0$ we also have $x_1 \geqslant 0$ and $x_2 \geqslant 0$.

(b) Adding slack variables r and s we obtain:

$$6x_1 + 2x_2 + r = 1$$

and $\qquad\qquad x_1 + 5x_2 + s = 1$

The steps in the simplex method are shown opposite.

Basic variable	x_1	x_2	r	s	Value	
r	⑥	2	1	0	1	←
s	1	5	0	1	1	
P	-1	-1	0	0	0	

↑

x_1	1	$\frac{1}{3}$	$\frac{1}{6}$	0	$\frac{1}{6}$
s	0	④$\frac{2}{3}$	$-\frac{1}{6}$	1	$\frac{5}{6}$
P	0	$-\frac{2}{3}$	$\frac{1}{6}$	0	$\frac{1}{6}$

(← on s row)

↑

x_1	1	0	$\frac{5}{28}$	$-\frac{1}{14}$	$\frac{3}{28}$
x_2	0	1	$-\frac{1}{28}$	$\frac{3}{14}$	$\frac{5}{28}$
P	0	0	$\frac{1}{7}$	$\frac{1}{7}$	$\frac{2}{7}$

This tableau is the optimal tableau.

So $\qquad x_1 = \frac{3}{28},\ x_2 = \frac{5}{28}$ and $P = \dfrac{1}{v} = \frac{2}{7}$

Hence:

$p_1 = x_1 v = \left(\frac{3}{28}\right)\left(\frac{7}{2}\right) = \frac{3}{8}$

$p_2 = x_2 v = \left(\frac{5}{28}\right)\left(\frac{7}{2}\right) = \frac{5}{8}$

and $\qquad v = \frac{7}{2} = 3\frac{1}{2}$

(c) If A chooses A_1 with probability q_1 and A_2 with probability q_2, then $q_1 + q_2 = 1$.

Also $\qquad\qquad\qquad 6q_1 + q_2 \geqslant v$

and $\qquad\qquad\qquad 2q_1 + 5q_2 \geqslant v$

If we write $y_1 = \dfrac{q_1}{v}$ and $y_2 = \dfrac{q_2}{v}$ then we obtain the linear programming problem to be solved to obtain A's strategy:

minimise $\qquad\qquad Q = y_1 + y_2$

subject to $\qquad\qquad 6y_1 + y_2 \geqslant 1$
$\qquad\qquad\qquad 2y_1 + 5y_2 \geqslant 1$
$\qquad\qquad\qquad y_1 \geqslant 0,\ y_2 \geqslant 0$

Since this is the dual of B's problem we can obtain its solution from the bottom row of optimal tableau above.
We have:

$\qquad\qquad y_1 = \frac{1}{7}$ and $y_2 = \frac{1}{7},\ Q = \dfrac{1}{v} = \frac{2}{7}$

So

$$q_1 = y_1 v = \left(\tfrac{1}{7}\right)\left(\tfrac{7}{2}\right) = \tfrac{1}{2}$$

$$q_2 = y_2 v = \left(\tfrac{1}{7}\right)\left(\tfrac{7}{2}\right) = \tfrac{1}{2} v = 3\tfrac{1}{2}$$

and

$$v = 3\tfrac{1}{2}$$

Revision exercise 4

1 Determine which of the following games has a saddle point:

(a)

3	4
7	6

(b)

1	−2	7
4	3	6
5	2	2

(c)

2	−1	6
1	3	4
3	4	2

(d)

1	3	2
4	2	6

2 In each of the following 2×2 games find:
  (i) the optimal strategies for both players
  (ii) the value of the game.

(a)

B

A	B_1	B_2
A_1	6	3
A_2	2	4

(b)

N

M	N_1	N_2
M_1	−2	1
M_2	2	−1

3 The payoff matrix for a zero-sum game, played by Annabel and Betty, is:

B

A	B_1	B_2	B_3
A_1	5	2	3
A_2	1	3	6

(a) Use the principle of dominance to reduce the payoff matrix.

(b) Hence obtain the optimal strategy for both players and the value of the game.

4 Find the optimal mixed strategies for both players when the payoff matrix is:

		Q	
		Q₁	**Q₂**
P	**P₁**	4	−1
	P₂	1	2
	P₃	3	1

You should solve the problem graphically by first considering player Q.

5

		B		
		B₁	**B₂**	**B₃**
A	**A₁**	2	3	1
	A₂	1	2	3
	A₃	3	1	2

For the payoff matrix given above:

(a) obtain the linear programming problem which when solved will give the optimal strategy for B

(b) solve the linear programming problem, using the simplex algorithm, to obtain B's optimal strategy and the value of the game.

(c) deduce the optimal strategy for A.

6

		D		
		D₁	**D₂**	**D₃**
C	**C₁**	2	3	−2
	C₂	−4	−1	−1
	C₃	−5	0	1

For the game given by the above payoff matrix determine the optimal strategy for both players and the value of the game. [Note that not all entries are positive. See page 88 of Heinemann Book D2.]

If your answer is incorrect:

1 Two large computer manufacturers, Alpha (A) and Beta (B), control the entire computer market in a given region. For the forthcoming model year they both have three options:

Review Heinemann Book D2
(a) pages 96–98
(b) pages 81–83

   1 make no changes
   2 make minor changes
   3 make major changes

The percentage changes in market share from the various combinations of these options are shown in the table below.

		B		
		B_1	B_2	B_3
	A_1	0	−5	−9
A	A_2	4	0	−6
	A_3	7	−2	0

(a) Reduce the payoff matrix by using the principle of dominance.
(b) Hence find:
   (i)   the strategy to be used by A
   (ii) the strategy to be used by B
   (iii) the value of the game.

2 The payoff matrix for a two person zero-sum game between Gareth and Katherine is:

Review Heinemann Book D2
(a) pages 96–98
(b) pages 84–87

		K		
		K_1	K_2	K_3
	G_1	2	4	3
G	G_2	5	2	6
	G_3	1	6	2

(a) Explain why Katherine will never use strategy K_3.
(b) After removing K_3, solve the zero-sum game given by the remaining payoff matrix using graphical methods. Give the fraction of time that Katherine will use strategies K_1 and K_2, and give the value of the game.
(c) Hence find the fraction of the time that Gareth will use strategies G_1, G_2 and G_3.

3 The payoff matrix for a two person zero-sum game is shown below:

Review Heinemann Book D2 pages 88–95

	Q		
R	3	−2	1
	1	3	2

(a) Explain why it is necessary to add 3 to each of the numbers in the matrix before one can solve it using the simplex method.

(b) For the new payoff matrix:

	Q		
R	6	1	4
	4	6	5

   (i)   obtain the linear programming problem which when solved will give the optimal strategy for Q

   (ii) solve the linear programming problem using the simplex method to obtain Q's optimal strategy and the value of the modified game

   (iii) deduce the optimal strategy for R.

(c) Hence write down the value of the game and the strategies of R and Q for the original game.

Test yourself answers

1 (a) A_2 dominates A_1

   B_2 dominates B_1

   Reduced payoff matrix is $\begin{pmatrix} 0 & -6 \\ -2 & 0 \end{pmatrix}$

(b) (i)   A should use: A_2 for $\frac{1}{4}$ of time   (ii)   B should use: B_2 for $\frac{3}{4}$ of time   (iii)   value of the game is -1.5

                              A_3 for $\frac{3}{4}$ of time B_3 for $\frac{1}{4}$ of time

                              never use A_1 never use B_1

2 (a)   If Katherine plays K_3 then whatever Gareth plays she will lose more than if she plays K_1 since $3 > 2$, $6 > 5$ and $2 > 1$.

(b)   Katherine will play K_1 for $\frac{1}{2}$ of the time and K_2 for $\frac{1}{2}$ of the time.

      Value of the game is $3\frac{1}{2}$.

(c)   Gareth will never play G_1

            play G_2 for $\frac{5}{8}$ of the time

            play G_3 for $\frac{3}{8}$ of the time

3 (a)   In formulating this as a linear programme we require the value v to be positive, as we divide the probabilities by it. The simplex method requires the decision variables to be non-negative. We can ensure the necessary conditions are satisfied by making all entries in the table positive; this is achieved by adding 3 to each.

(b) (i)   Maximise $x_1 + x_2 + x_3$

            subject to $6x_1 + x_2 + 4x_3 \leqslant 1$

                        $4x_1 + 6x_2 + 5x_3 \leqslant 1$

                        $x_1 \geqslant 0, x_2 \geqslant 0, x_3 \geqslant 0$

   (ii) $x_1 = \frac{5}{32}, x_2 = \frac{1}{16}, \frac{1}{v} = \frac{7}{32}$

            $p_1 = \frac{5}{7}, p_2 = \frac{2}{7}, p_3 = 0, v = 4\frac{4}{7}$

   (iii)   R should use R_1 for $\frac{2}{7}$ of the time and R_2 for $\frac{5}{7}$ of the time

            So Q should use strategy Q_1 for $\frac{5}{7}$ of the time, Q_2 for $\frac{2}{7}$ of the time and never use Q_3.

(c)   The value of the original game is $4\frac{4}{7} - 3 = 1\frac{4}{7}$

      R should use R_1 for $\frac{2}{7}$ of the time

                  R_2 for $\frac{5}{7}$ of the time

      Q should use Q_1 for $\frac{5}{7}$ of the time

                  Q_2 for $\frac{2}{7}$ of the time

                  never use Q_3

Dynamic programming 5

Example 1

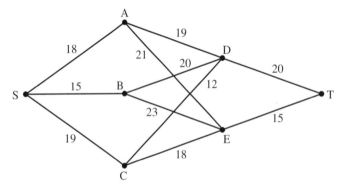

The above diagram shows the road network in a certain area. The weights on the edges give the distances, in km, between the various towns.

(a) Set up and use a dynamic programming tabulation to find the shortest route from S to T.
(b) Find, from your tabulation, the shortest route from S to T that uses the road SA.

Answer

(a) T is a stage 0 vertex.
D and E are stage 1 vertices.
A, B and C are stage 2 vertices.
S is a stage 3 vertex.

The dynamic programming tabulation is then:

Stage	Initial state	Action	Destination	Value
1	D	DT	T	20*
	E	ET	T	15*
2	A	AD	D	$19 + 20 = 39$
		AE	E	$21 + 15 = 36^*$
	B	BD	D	$20 + 20 = 40$
		BE	E	$23 + 15 = 38^*$
	C	CD	D	$12 + 20 = 32^*$
		CE	E	$18 + 15 = 33$
3	S	SA	A	$18 + 36 = 54$
		SB	B	$15 + 38 = 53$
		SC	C	$19 + 32 = 51^*$

* indicates the **smallest** value as we are looking for the **shortest** route. Hence the shortest route from S to T is of length 51 km. Reading up the table the edges on the shortest route are SC, CD and DT, and the route is S → C → D → T.

(b) The shortest route that uses SA is again found from the table and is S → A → E → T, length 54 km.

Example 2

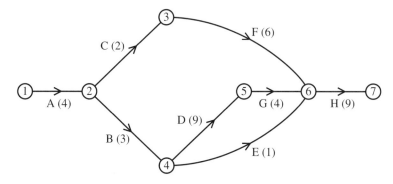

The diagram above shows an activity network in which the activities are modelled by edges. The weights on the edges give the duration of the activities in days. The longest path through this network from vertex 1 to vertex 7 gives the critical path and the length of this path gives the critical time.

(a) Label the vertices with (stage; state) variables.
(b) Use dynamic programming to find the longest route from vertex 1 to vertex 7.
(c) Hence write down the critical activities and the critical path and its length.

Answer

(a) ⑦ is the only stage 0 vertex and so is (0; 1)

⑥ is the only stage 1 vertex and so is (1; 1)

⑤ is the only stage 2 vertex and so is (2; 1)

③ and ④ are stage 3 vertices and so we have ③ as (3; 1) and ④ as (3; 2)

② is the only stage 4 vertex and so is (4; 1)

① is the only stage 5 vertex and so is (5; 1)

(b) The dynamic programming tabulation for this problem is shown below. The * indicate the **largest** value here as we are looking for the **longest** path.

Stage	Initial state	Action	Destination	Value
1	(1; 1)	H(9)	(0; 1)	9*
2	(2; 1)	G(4)	(1; 1)	4 + 9 = 13*
3	(3; 1)	F(6)	(1; 1)	6 + 9 = 15*
	(3; 2)	E(1)	(1; 1)	1 + 9 = 10
		D(9)	(2; 1)	9 + 13 = 22*
4	(4; 1)	B(3)	(3; 2)	3 + 22 = 25*
		C(2)	(3; 1)	2 + 15 = 17
5	(5; 1)	A(4)	(4; 1)	4 + 25 = 29*

The longest route is of length 29.

Reading up the table, the edges (activities) on this longest path are A, B, D, G, H.

(c) The critical activities are A, B, D, G and H. The critical path is:

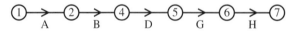

and is of length 29 days.

Example 3

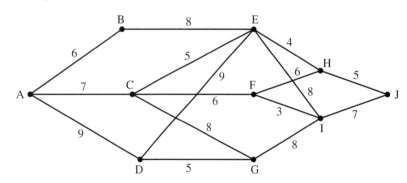

The organisers of a safari rally drew up the above diagram showing possible stopping points A, B, C, ..., J and the roads between them. The distances are given in miles. They wish to plan a route from A to J such that the longest leg between two stops is as short as possible, so as to minimise the amount of fuel that needs to be carried. Use dynamic programming to find this minimax route. State the length of the longest leg on this route.

Answer

Stage 0   vertex: J

      1   vertices: H and I

      2   vertices: E, F and G

      3   vertices: B, C and D

      4   vertex: A

Stage	Initial state	Action	Destination	Value
1	H	HJ	J	5*
	I	IJ	J	7*
2	E	EH	H	max(4, 5) = 5*
		EI	I	max(8, 7) = 8
	F	FH	H	max(6, 5) = 6*
		FI	I	max(3, 7) = 7
	G	GI	I	max(8, 7) = 8*
3	B	BE	E	max(8, 5) = 8*
	C	CE	E	max(5, 5) = 5*
		CF	F	max(6, 6) = 6
		CG	G	max(8, 8) = 8
	D	DE	E	max(9, 5) = 9
		DG	G	max(5, 8) = 8*
4	A	AB	B	max(6, 8) = 8
		AC	C	max(7, 5) = 7*
		AD	D	max(9, 8) = 9

* indicates current minimax.

The route on which the longest leg is as short as possible uses edges AC, CE, EH and HJ, that is ACEHJ.

The length of the longest leg on this route is 7 miles.

Example 4

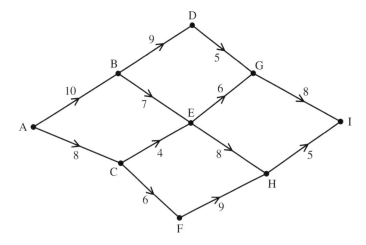

The above network models possible production lines starting at A and finishing at I. The weights on the edges are the production rates. The production manager wishes to determine the path for which the slowest leg is as fast as possible. Find this maximin path using dynamic programming.

Answer

Stage	0	vertex:	I
	1	vertices:	G and H
	2	vertices:	D, E and F
	3	vertices:	B and C
	4	vertex:	A

Stage	Initial state	Action	Destination	Value
1	G	GI	I	8*
	H	HI	I	5*
2	D	DG	G	min(5, 8) = 5*
	E	EG	G	min(6, 8) = 6*
		EH	H	min(8, 5) = 5
	F	FH	H	min(9, 5) = 5*
3	B	BD	D	min(9, 5) = 5
		BE	E	min(7, 6) = 6*
	C	CE	E	min(4, 6) = 4
		CF	F	min(6, 5) = 5*
4	A	AB	B	min(10, 6) = 6*
		AC	C	min(8, 5) = 5

* indicates current maximin.

Hence the maximin route is AB, BE, EG and GI, and the slowest leg on this route is EG on which the rate is 6.

Example 5

Forest Products makes three types of garden shed and has orders for one shed of each type. They wish to make them in the order that will maximise profits. The profits made depend on the order in which the sheds are made and are shown below.

Profit in £s

Already made	A	B	C
None	58	75	70
A	—	70	90
B	60	—	80
C	65	75	—
A and B	—	—	80
A and C	—	85	—
B and C	70	—	—

(a) Model the data in the table by a network in which the vertices represent the sheds made.
(b) Use dynamic programming to determine the order in which the sheds should be made to maximise the profit.

Answer

(a) The network that models this situation is shown below, together with the (stage; state) variables.

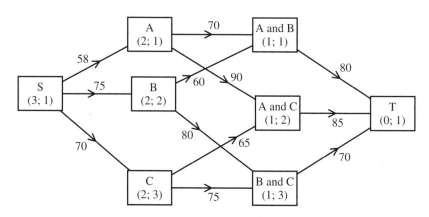

Here S = none made and T = all made.
(b) The dynamic programming tabulation to find the longest route corresponding to the maximum profit is shown on the next page.

Stage	Initial state	Action	Destination	Value
1	(1; 1)	Make C	T (0; 1)	80*
	(1; 2)	Make B	T (0; 1)	85*
	(1; 3)	Make A	T (0; 1)	70*
2	A (2; 1)	Make B	(1; 1)	70 + 80 = 150
		Make C	(1; 2)	90 + 85 = 175*
	B (2; 2)	Make A	(1; 1)	60 + 80 = 140
		Make C	(1; 3)	80 + 70 = 150*
	C (2; 3)	Make A	(1; 2)	65 + 85 = 150*
		Make B	(1; 3)	75 + 70 = 145
3	S (3; 1)	Make A	(2; 1)	58 + 175 = 233*
		Make B	(2; 2)	75 + 150 = 225
		Make C	(2; 3)	70 + 150 = 220

The maximum profit that can be made is £233. The order in which the sheds should be made is A then C then B.

Revision exercise 5

1

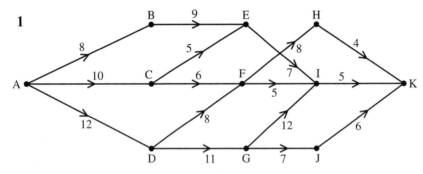

For the network given above find:

(a) the shortest route from A to K

(b) the longest route from A to K

(c) the maximin route from A to K

(d) the minimax route from A to K.

2

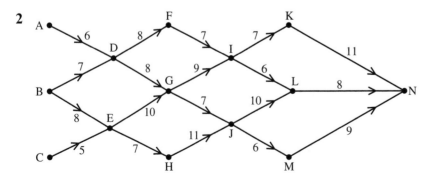

The diagram opposite shows a network of roads with the distances given in km. Afzal wishes to start at either A or B or C and travel to N. He wishes to travel a minimum distance.

(a) Use dynamic programming to find the shortest routes from each of A, B and C to N.

(b) Hence determine which route Afzal should take.

3

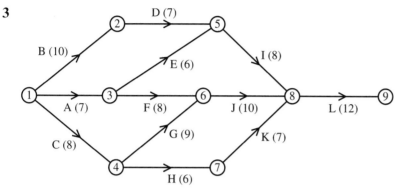

The diagram above shows an activity network in which the activities are modelled by edges. The weights on the edges give the durations of the activities in hours.

Use dynamic programming to find the longest path from ① to ⑨ and hence obtain the critical activities, the critical path and the length of the critical path.

4 Jim Smith is planning to build three new buildings, A, B and C, at the rate of one per year. His estimates of the costs are shown in the table below, in units of £1000.

Cost (in units of £1000)

Already built	A	B	C
None	80	60	70
A	—	70	65
B	75	—	70
C	70	65	—
A and **B**	—	—	55
A and **C**	—	60	—
B and **C**	75	—	—

For tax reasons it is advantageous to arrange the sequence of building so that the least annual cost is as large as possible. Determine the order in which Jim should build the buildings.

If your answer is incorrect:

1

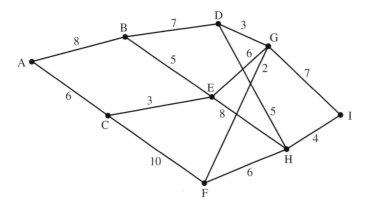

Review Heinemann Book D2 pages 108–112

The weights on the edges of the above network give the maximum weight (in tonnes) of a lorry allowed on the road modelled by that edge, due to weight limits on bridges.
Use dynamic programming to find the weight of the heaviest lorry that can travel from A to I. Give the route it must take.

2

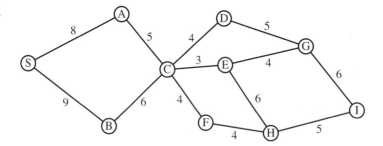

Review Heinemann Book D2 pages 102–106

The network above shows locations of interest in a country park and the possible paths between them. The distances are given in km. Penelope wishes to go from S to I by the shortest route.
Use dynamic programming to show that there are two shortest routes and give the length of these routes.

3

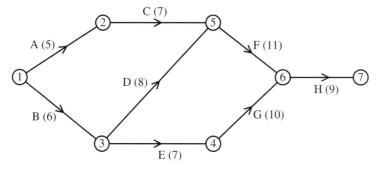

The diagram above shows an activity network that models a building project. The activities are modelled by the edges and the weights give the duration of the activities in weeks.

(a) Use dynamic programming to find the longest path from ① to ⑦.

(b) Hence obtain the critical activities, the critical path and its length.

Review Heinemann Book D2 pages 106–107

Test yourself answers

1 Maximin weight is 5 tonnes, route ABEGI
2 SACEGI and SACFHI, length = 26 km
3 **(a)** Longest path is ①—→③—→⑤—→⑥—→⑦
  (b) Critical activities are B, D, F and H
  Critical path is BDFH, length = 34 weeks

Examination style paper

Attempt **all** questions. **Time: 90 minutes**

1   A plant has four operators to be assigned to four machines. The time, in minutes, required by each worker to produce a product on each machine is shown in the table below.

Machine

		A	**B**	**C**	**D**
	1	12	14	11	13
	2	7	12	9	10
Operator	**3**	14	16	15	13
	4	10	17	13	11

The plant manager wishes to make the assignment of operator to machine so as to keep the total time to a minimum.

Formulate this as a linear programming problem explaining how you obtain the objective function and the constraints.   **(6 marks)**

2   Four taxis, A, B, C and D, are available and there are four customers, 1, 2, 3 and 4, requiring taxis. The distances between the taxis and customers are shown in the table below, in kilometres. The taxi company wishes to assign the taxis to customers so that the total distance travelled is a minimum.

Customer

		1	**2**	**3**	**4**
	A	14	5	8	7
	B	5	15	9	8
Taxi	**C**	8	9	4	10
	D	7	9	11	15

Use the Hungarian algorithm to obtain an optimal assignment and find the minimum total distance.   **(9 marks)**

3   Jeremy lives at A and wishes to spend a weekend at one of H, I and J. He wishes to use a minimum amount of petrol on his journey. The diagram opposite shows the possible routes available to him. The weights on the edges give the amount of petrol, in litres, used on that road.

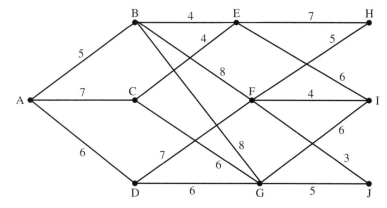

(a) Use dynamic programming to determine:
   (i)   the place at which Jeremy should spend the weekend
   (ii) the route he should take
   (iii) the amount of petrol he will use on that route.   **(10 marks)**
(b) Jeremy decides he wishes to visit D on his journey. Determine at which of H, I and J he will now spend his weekend, the route he will take and the total amount of petrol he will use.   **(3 marks)**

4

	A	B	C	D	E
A	—	132	217	164	58
B	132	—	290	201	79
C	217	290	—	113	303
D	164	201	113	—	196
E	58	79	303	196	—

A commercial traveller, Jacky, needs to visit stores in five cities, A, B, C, D and E. The table above gives the distances, in km, between these five cities. Jacky lives in city A and plans a route starting and finishing at A. She wishes to visit each city and drive the minimum distance.

(a) Starting from A, use Prim's algorithm to obtain a minimum spanning tree. State the order in which you selected the arcs and draw the tree.   **(5 marks)**
(b) (i)   Using your answer to (a) determine an initial upper bound for the length of the route planned by Jacky.
   (ii) Starting from your initial upper bound and using at least one shortcut obtain a route that is less than 710 km.   **(4 marks)**
(c) Using the nearest neighbour algorithm and starting at A obtain an upper bound for the length of Jacky's route.   **(2 marks)**
(d) Can you find a shorter tour than you found in (c) by using the nearest neighbour algorithm starting at a vertex other than A? If so, give this route.   **(3 marks)**

5 Two players, A and B, play a zero-sum game. The payoff matrix for the game is shown below.

	B I	II
A **I**	30	60
II	50	10
III	32	32

(a) Obtain, by graphical methods, the optimal strategy of player B and the value of the game. **(10 marks)**

(b) Hence obtain the optimal strategy of player A. **(5 marks)**

6 A soft drinks producer has two factories at Archfield and Brambleford. They can supply the following number of cases of lemonade per month:

Factory	No. of cases
Archfield	2400
Brambleford	2000

The lemonade is to be transported to three distributers, whose monthly demands are:

Distributor	No. of cases
Thurnby	1800
Northtown	1500
Mineacre	1600

The producer must pay the following shipping costs per crate, in pence:

	T	N	M
A	35	60	50
B	65	40	25

He wishes to ship the crates with minimum total cost.

(a) Show that this is an unbalanced transportation problem and produce a corresponding balanced problem. **(4 marks)**

(b) Write down the north-west corner solution and show that it is not optimal. **(6 marks)**

(c) Use the stepping-stone method to obtain an improved solution. **(3 marks)**

(d) Show that the improved solution obtained in **(c)** is optimal. **(2 marks)**

(e) Interpret the solution found in **(c)**. **(3 marks)**

Answers

Revision exercise 1

1 **(a)**

40	20	20
		50
		10

(b)

20		
30		
40	20	10

(c)

15		
10	15	10
		20

2 1000

3 **(a)** Improvement indices are all non-negative, 1, 2, 3 and 0, cost 970.

(b)

20		
10	20	
60		10

4 **(a)** There is a negative improvement index (-1).

(b)

15		
10		25
	15	5

cost = 595

5 **(a)** Number of turkeys available
$$= 25 + 45 + 60 = 130$$
Number of turkeys required $= 50 + 50 = 100$
Surplus $= 130 - 100$, therefore unbalanced.

	S_1	S_2	Dummy	Available
F_1	3	5	0	25
F_2	6	4	0	45
F_3	7	7	0	60
Demand	50	50	30	

(b) North-west corner solution

25		
25	20	
	30	30

Optimal solution

25		
	45	
25	5	30

cost = 465

(c) Farm F_3 'sends' 30 to the dummy supermarket in this solution and so does not distribute all its turkeys, in fact it only distributes 30 turkeys.

6

10	10	
	5	
		12

minimum mileage = 619

7 **(a)**

4	3	
	2	3
		3

(b)

4		3
	5	
		3

or

1		6
	5	
3		

cost = 50

8 Let x_{ij} be the number of units sent from source S_i to destination D_j.

Minimise cost $C = 5x_{11} + 2x_{12} + 2x_{13} + 7x_{21}$
$+ 3x_{22} + 4x_{23} + 6x_{31} + 4x_{32} + 3x_{33}$
subject to $x_{11} + x_{12} + x_{13} = 7$
$x_{21} + x_{22} + x_{23} = 5$
$x_{31} + x_{32} + x_{33} = 3$
$x_{11} + x_{21} + x_{31} = 4$
$x_{12} + x_{22} + x_{32} = 5$
$x_{13} + x_{23} + x_{33} = 6$
$x_{ij} \geqslant 0$ ($i = 1, 2, 3$ and $j = 1, 2, 3$)

Revision exercise 2

1 P → 2   cost 9
R → 1   cost 7
S → 3   cost 6
Minimum total cost = £22 000

2 A → 1   21
B → 3   24
C → 4   26
D → 2   21
Minimum time = 92 minutes

3 Shoes → 3   22
Toys → 2   26
Auto → 4   28
Housewares → 1   24
Maximum profit = £100 000

4 (i)   1 → B   200
2 → C   260
3 → A   270
4 → D   200
Cost = £930
(ii)   1 → B   200
2 → A   220
3 → C   310
4 → D   200
Cost = £930

5 A → 3   29
B → 2   39
C → 1   33
Total time = 101 hours
D does not get a job.

6 Let $x_{ij} = \begin{cases} 1 & \text{if accountant } i \text{ is allocated} \\ & \text{to project } j \\ 0 & \text{otherwise} \end{cases}$

Minimum $= 15x_{P1} + 9x_{P2} + 12x_{P3}$
$+ 7x_{R1} + 5x_{R2} + 10x_{R3}$
$+ 13x_{S1} + 4x_{S2} + 6x_{S3}$
Subject to $x_{P1} + x_{P2} + x_{P3} = 1$
$x_{R1} + x_{R2} + x_{R3} = 1$
$x_{S1} + x_{S2} + x_{S3} = 1$
$x_{P1} + x_{R1} + x_{S1} = 1$
$x_{P2} + x_{R2} + x_{S2} = 1$
$x_{P3} + x_{R3} + x_{S3} = 1$

Revision exercise 3

1 **(a)**

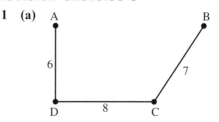

Upper bound = $2 \times (21) = 42$
(b) Use shortcut BA instead of BCDA.
Upper bound is then $42 - 11 = 31$.

2 **(a)**

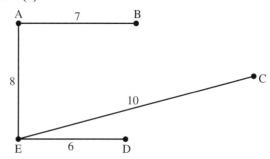

Upper bound = $2 \times (31) = 62$
(b) Use shortcut BC instead of BAEC. This gives a saving of $25 - 14 = 11$. Upper bound is then $62 - 11 = 51$.

3 **(a)**

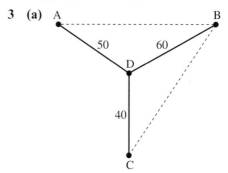

Initial upper bound $= 2 \times (150) = 300$

(b) Use shortcuts AB and BC, as shown. We then reduce the upper bound by

$(50 + 60) - 92 = 18$ and $(60 + 40) - 85 = 15$.

Total reduction $= 33$.

New upper bound is 267.

4 *Question 1*

    (a) $15 + 9 + 6 = 30$

    (b) Remove B $(8 + 6) + (10 + 7) = 31$

        or remove C $(6 + 10) + (7 + 8) = 31$

  Question 2

    (a) $28 + 8 + 7 = 43$

    (b) Remove C $(8 + 7 + 6) + (10 + 14) = 45$

        or remove D $(7 + 8 + 10) + (6 + 13) = 44$

        or remove E $(7 + 13 + 14) + (6 + 8) = 48$

  Question 3

    (a) $100 + 50 + 80 = 230$

    (b) Remove B $(50 + 40) + (60 + 85) = 235$

        or remove D $(80 + 85) + (40 + 50) = 255$

5 *Question 1*

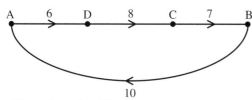

Upper bound $= 31$

  Question 2

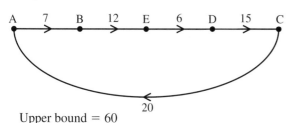

Upper bound $= 60$

  Question 3

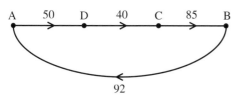

Upper bound $= 267$

6 Starting at E:

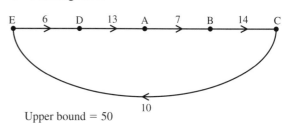

Upper bound $= 50$

7 **(a)**

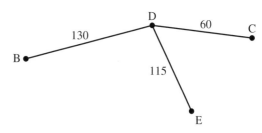

  (b) Initial upper bound

      $= 2 \times (60 + 60 + 80 + 85) = 570$ miles

  (c) Using BC instead of BADC saves

  $(60 + 60 + 85) - 135 = 70$ miles

      Using DE instead of DAE saves

      $(60 + 80) - 115 = 25$ miles

      New upper bound

      $= 570 - 70 - 25 = 475$ miles

  (d) When A is removed the minimum spanning tree is:

The two shortest edges incident at A are AD (60) and AE (80), so a lower bound is

$(60 + 115 + 130) + (60 + 80) = 445$ miles

  (e) Length of optimal route L satisfies

$445 \leqslant L \leqslant 475$

  (f) A route satisfying this is ABCDEA, length 475

8 (a)

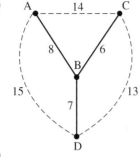

(b)

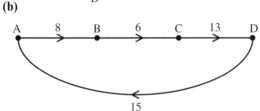

Length = 42

Tour = ABCDA

(c) In the original network the tour is

ABCBDBA

9 (a)

	A	B	C	D	E
A	—	4	10	13	5
B	4	—	6	14	6
C	10	6	—	9	7
D	13	14	9	—	8
E	5	6	7	8	—

(b)

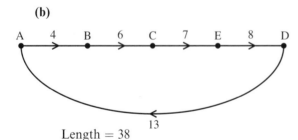

Length = 38

In the original network the tour is

ABCEDEA

(c) For example,

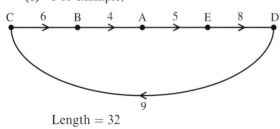

Length = 32

Tour = CBAEDC

Revision exercise 4

1 (a) Yes, 6

(b) Yes, 3

(c) No

(d) No

2 (a) (i) A should play A_1 for fraction $\frac{2}{5}$ of time

A_2 for fraction $\frac{3}{5}$ of time

B should play B_1 for fraction $\frac{1}{5}$ of time

B_2 for fraction $\frac{4}{5}$ of time

(ii) Value of game is $3\frac{3}{5}$

(b) (i) M should play

M_1 for fraction $\frac{1}{2}$ of time

M_2 for fraction $\frac{1}{2}$ of time

N should play

N_1 for fraction $\frac{1}{3}$ of time

N_2 for fraction $\frac{2}{3}$ of time

(ii) Value of game is 0

3 (a) The payoff matrix may be reduced to:

5	2
1	3

since B_3 is dominated by B_2 ($2 < 3$ and

$3 < 6$).

(b) A should play A_1 for fraction $\frac{2}{5}$ of time

A_2 for fraction $\frac{3}{5}$ of time

B should play B_1 for fraction $\frac{1}{5}$ of time

B_2 for fraction $\frac{4}{5}$ of time

Value of the game is $2\frac{3}{5}$

4 Q should play Q_1 for $\frac{1}{3}$ of time

Q_2 for $\frac{2}{3}$ of time

P should play P_2 for $\frac{2}{3}$ of time

P_3 for $\frac{1}{3}$ of time

and never play P_1

Value of the game $1\frac{2}{3}$

5 (a) Maximise $P = \dfrac{1}{v} = x_1 + x_2 + x_3$

subject to $2x_1 + 3x_2 + x_3 \leqslant 1$

$x_1 + 2x_2 + 3x_3 \leqslant 1$

$3x_1 + x_2 + 2x_3 \leqslant 1$

$x_1, x_2, x_3 \geqslant 0$

(b) $x_1 = \frac{1}{6}$, $x_2 = \frac{1}{6}$, $x_3 = \frac{1}{6}$, $P = \frac{1}{2}$

So $v = 2$, $p_1 = p_2 = p_3 = \frac{1}{3}$

So B should use each strategy for $\frac{1}{3}$ of the time.

(c) $y_1 = \frac{1}{6}$, $y_2 = \frac{1}{6}$, $y_3 = \frac{1}{6}$, $\frac{1}{v} = \frac{1}{2}$

So $v = 2$, $q_1 = q_2 = q_3 = \frac{1}{3}$

So A should use each strategy for $\frac{1}{3}$ of the time.

6 The payoff matrix may be reduced by the principle of dominance to:

2	-2
-4	-1
-5	1

Solving graphically: D should use D_1 for a fraction $\frac{3}{10}$ of the time, D_2 never, D_3 for $\frac{7}{10}$ of the time. The value of the game is $-\frac{4}{5}$.

C should use C_1 for $\frac{3}{5}$ of the time, C_2 never and C_3 for $\frac{2}{5}$ of the time.

Revision exercise 5

1 (a) ACFIK, length $= 26$

(b) ADGIK, length $= 40$

(c) ADGJK, minimum leg on this route is $JK = 6$

(d) ABEIK, maximum leg on this route is $BE = 9$

2 (a) ADFILN, length $= 35$

BDFILN, length $= 36$

CEGJMN, length $= 37$

(b) Afzal should take route ADFILN.

3 ①⟶④⟶⑥⟶⑧⟶⑨,

length $= 39$

Critical activities C, G, J, L

Critical path

①⟶④⟶⑥⟶⑧⟶⑨

length $= 39$ hours

4 C then B then A (smallest annual cost is then £65 000)

Examination style paper

1 $x_{ij} = 1$ if operator i is assigned to machine j

$= 0$ otherwise

Minimise $Z = 12x_{1A} + 14x_{1B} + 11x_{1C} + 13x_{1D}$
$+ 7x_{2A} + 12x_{2B} + 9x_{2C} + 10x_{2D}$
$+ 14x_{3A} + 16x_{3B} + 15x_{3C} + 13x_{3D}$
$+ 10x_{4A} + 17x_{4B} + 13x_{4C} + 11x_{4D}$

Total time obtained by adding the product of x_{ij} and t_{ij} for each cell.

$$x_{1A} + x_{1B} + x_{1C} + x_{1D} = 1$$
$$x_{2A} + x_{2B} + x_{2C} + x_{2D} = 1$$
$$x_{3A} + x_{3B} + x_{3C} + x_{3D} = 1$$
$$x_{4A} + x_{4B} + x_{4C} + x_{4D} = 1$$

Each operator will be assigned to a machine.

$$x_{1A} + x_{2A} + x_{3A} + x_{4A} = 1$$
$$x_{1B} + x_{2B} + x_{3B} + x_{4B} = 1$$
$$x_{1C} + x_{2C} + x_{3C} + x_{4C} = 1$$
$$x_{1D} + x_{2D} + x_{3D} + x_{4D} = 1$$

Each machine will be assigned to an operator.

2 $A \to 2$, $B \to 4$, $C \to 3$, $D \to 1$

Minimum total distance $= 24\,\text{km}$

3 (a) (i) I **(ii)** ABEI **(iii)** 15 litres

(b) J, route ADFJ, 16 litres used

4 (a)

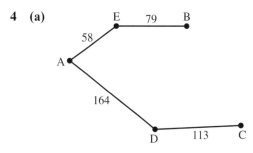

AE, EB, AD, DC

(b) (i) 828 km

(ii) Use shortcut BC

AEBCDA, of length 704 km

(c) AEBDCA, of length 668 km

(d) There is no shorter route. DCAEBD has same length.

5 (a) B plays strategy I for $\frac{5}{7}$ of the time and strategy II for $\frac{2}{7}$ of the time

Value of the game is $38\frac{4}{7}$

(b) A plays strategy I for $\frac{3}{7}$ of the time, strategy II for $\frac{4}{7}$ of the time and never plays strategy III

6 (a) Demand 4900, available 4400

	T	M	N	Available
A	35	60	50	2400
B	65	40	25	2000
Dummy	0	0	0	500
Demand	1800	1500	1600	4900

(b) North-west corner solution

1800	600	
	900	1100
		500

Not optimal as $I_{32} = -15$

(c) Improved solution

1800	600	
	400	1600
	500	

(d) All improvement indices now positive

(e) A $\rightarrow$ T (1800)

A $\rightarrow$ N (600)

B $\rightarrow$ N (400)

B $\rightarrow$ M (1600)

So T gets his 1800, N only gets 1000 (500 short), M gets 1600.

Cost of this pattern is £1550